THE UNORTHODOX

HAGGADAH

THE UNORTHODOX HAGGADAH

A DOGMA-FREE PASSOVER FOR JEWS & OTHER CHOSEN PEOPLE

WRITTEN BY NATHAN PHILLIPS, JEW
DESIGNED BY JESSICA STEWART, GOY

Andrews McMeel Publishing

Kansas City • Sydney • London

SAFE FOR NON-BELIEVERS!

*For Victoria & Louisiana, the
finest Jewesses in all the world.*

BRUCHIM HABA'IM!
ברוכים הבאים!

FROM THE AUTHOR:

PEOPLE CALL ME RUDE · I WISH WE WERE ALL NUDE
I WISH THERE WAS NO BLACK AND WHITE · I WISH THERE WERE NO RULES
—PRINCE

I don't believe God exists. But, it's cool that some people do. Because, real or imagined, God has inspired some amazing stuff. Like gospel, mandalas, and the preachers who get bitten by snakes on purpose. But, He/She is also responsible for the worst stuff ever. Like torture, racism, homophobia, and the decline of MC Hammer's rap career.

I wrote *The Unorthodox Haggadah* for people who want to participate in weird rituals, without the hassle of dogma. Besides, if there is a God, he doesn't want you to follow rules. He wants you to soul clap and battle with swords. To buy the velvet painting of Black Jesus at the flea market because it's sexy, and eat pork when the mood hits you. Whether you think we are a divine vision or a happy accident, everybody loves to party. And the rituals we create are a testament to the creativity of the human race. Zealots shouldn't get to have all the fun.

This book is a celebration of those creations. It's about drinking wine and having a communal experience with Jews, Pagans, Buddhists, Satanists, and all their friends. Passover is a perfect holiday to use as a framework for such a celebration. The rules of the day are simple: "Ask Questions. Tell a Story." And every aspect of the meal from what you eat to how you sit is designed to help you do just that.

So, please understand this is not meant to be disrespectful. It's fully functional as a haggadah and it's wide open to interpretation. To discuss the big mysteries you have to ask big questions. So, tonight, let's see what happens when we stop following the rules and get weird.

TO BE READ BY THE HOST:

Welcome everyone. I'm your host, Dave. That may or may not be my actual name, but that's not important right now. What is important is this book. It's called a haggadah. It's an instruction manual for tonight's gathering. So, unless we want tonight's dinner party to devolve into some sort of drunken chit-chatty bacchanalia with lots of side talk and bad jokes, hear me now. Tonight is a conversation. So we all have to listen. This is not a normal night. It's better than that. So get into it.

Say "I promise to get into it." (They say it.)

Some parts are silly, some parts are serious.

Ask questions, but keep it moving.

If you get lost it's my job to get us back on track. I should have a conch shell or large staff in my hand right now. If I don't, use your imagination. Thank you.
While we eat we can all discuss what we loved and what we hated, but until then, let's crack open *The Unorthodox Haggadah* and get started.

FOR HELP SETTING UP, SEE PAGE 77.

These icons will help guide you through the meal. They'll tell you what needs to be read out loud, what should be enjoyed silently, and what requires a little participation. Take a second to study these. This is important.

NEXT READER

ACTION

KEEP IT TO YOURSELF

SHAREABLE MOMENT

🗨 WE WILL NOW DRAW A PICTURE.

📢 EVERYONE MAKE SURE YOU HAVE A WRITING UTENSIL. NOW CLOSE YOUR EYES. WHAT DO YOU PICTURE, WHEN I SAY "GOD"?

📢 NOW, DRAW THAT IN THE BOX TO THE RIGHT. WHEN YOU ARE DONE, PLACE YOUR PENCIL DOWN AND WAIT FOR EVERYONE TO FINISH.

THIS IS WHERE GOD GOES.

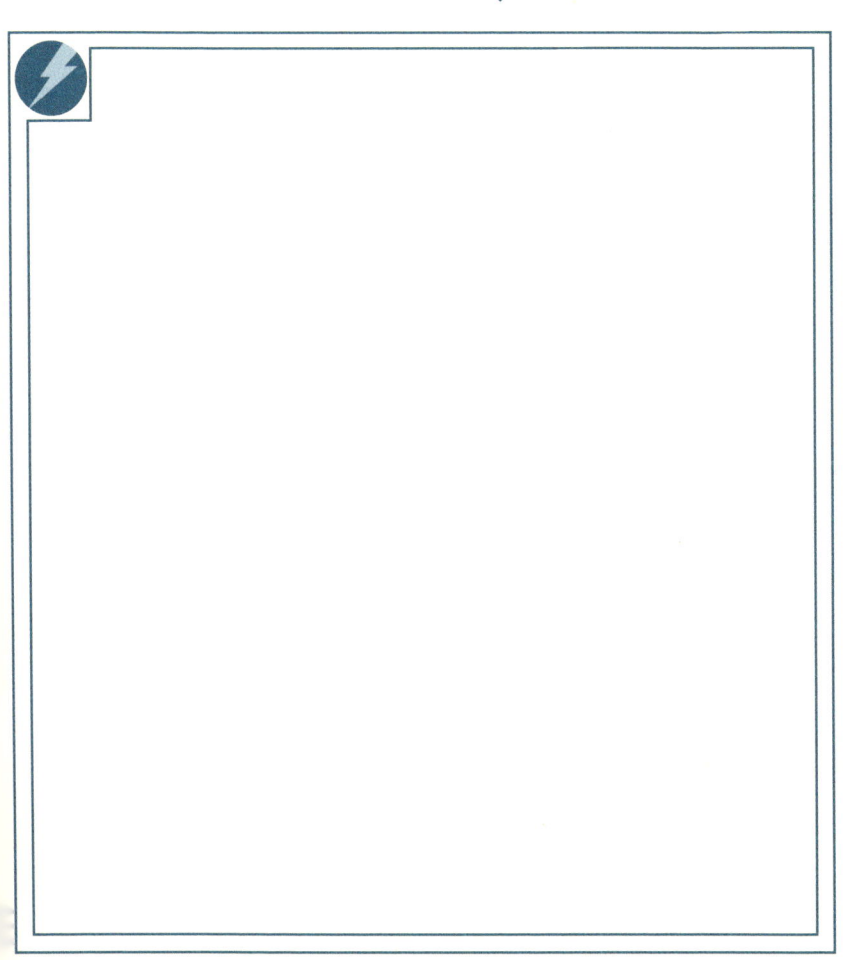

GOOD WORK! SHOW EVERYONE YOUR SKETCH NOW.

It doesn't matter if you think God is an old man with a beard, a Wiccan Stevie Nicks, or a blank box with nothing in it. Whatever you believe, please remember that everything is up for interpretation tonight and we all suck at drawing.

LET'S MAKE A GONG NOISE
AND WE CAN GET STARTED.

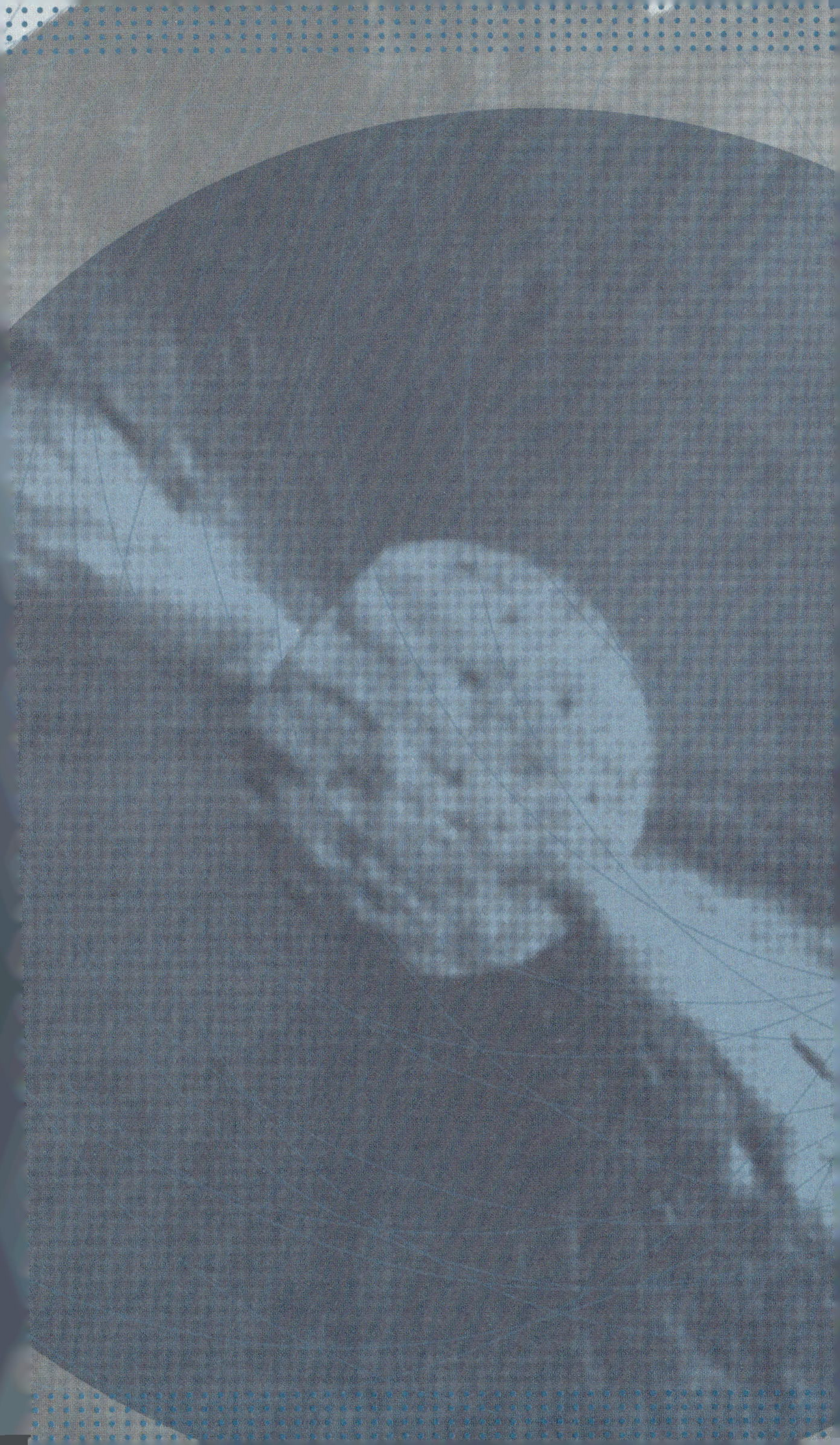

CANDLE LIGHTING
הדלקת נרות

CANDLE LIGHTING / הדלקת נרות

Let's get started.

Jews love lighting candles as much as Catholics love burning incense (and sometimes Jews).

Let's light some candles to mark the beginning of Passover. If it feels romantic, just go with it.

THE HOST SHOULD LIGHT THE CANDLES NOW.

Baruch atah Adonai Eloheinu melech ha'olam, asher kideshanu b'mitzvotav, v'tzivanu l'hadlik ner shel yom tov.

Translation: Candles are just lovely. (This is proof that God is female, because women love giving each other candles.)

SHEHECHEYANU / שההחינו

This next prayer is for special occasions. No one knows who owns the rights to this stuff.

Baruch atah Adonai Eloheinu melech ha'olam, shehecheyanu v'kiy'manu v'higiyanu lazman hazeh.

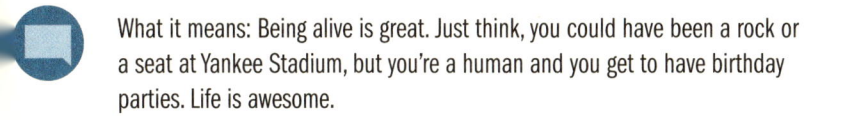

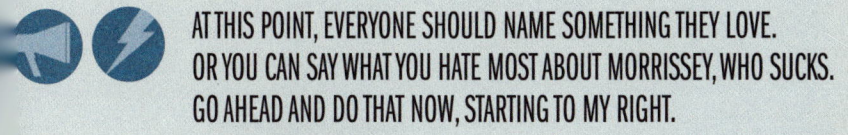

What it means: Being alive is great. Just think, you could have been a rock or a seat at Yankee Stadium, but you're a human and you get to have birthday parties. Life is awesome.

AT THIS POINT, EVERYONE SHOULD NAME SOMETHING THEY LOVE. OR YOU CAN SAY WHAT YOU HATE MOST ABOUT MORRISSEY, WHO SUCKS. GO AHEAD AND DO THAT NOW, STARTING TO MY RIGHT.

FUN FACTS PAGE / סדר = SEDER = ORDER

What is a Seder?
Seder is the Hebrew word for Order.
That's because we're here to tell a story in order from the beginning to the end, which is how stories used to be prior to the invention of the sequel.
We'll tell a story, eat from that plate in the center of the table, and sing songs. This is not about God. If it was about God, there would be more dancing.

Here's the run of show.

CANDLES AND SHECHIYANU

1. Kiddish: The First cup of wine

2. Urchatz: The First hand washing

3. Karpas: The First dipping

4. Yachatz: Breaking of the middle matzoh

5. Maggid: The storytelling section

6. Rachtzah: The Second hand washing (We're skipping this)

7. Motzi Matzoh: Blessings over the matzoh

8. Maror: The Second dipping

9. Korech: How to make a Hillel sandwich

10. Shulchan Orech: We enjoy a festive meal

11. Tzafun: Find the Afikoman

12. Hallel: Psalms of praise

13. Nirtzah: Conclusion

KIDDISH: THE FIRST CUP / כוס ראשון

Let's do this.
We begin by drinking the blood of a virgin lamb off the tip of a flaming golden scimitar.

In the event that you've de-virginized your lamb or misplaced your scimitar, use wine.

The first of the four officially mandated cups of wine you'll be drinking tonight is called the Cup of Sanctification.

Give it up for the Cup of Sanctification, y'all.
It's full of rich red wine, the official beverage of kings everywhere.

This intentionally bourgeois beverage reminds us that we are here tonight to celebrate the fact that we are free, and not stuck in a factory making Air Jordans. We are free to live as kings and queens and transgendered royalty!

Apologies to anyone at the table who has an uncle in prison or something.

EVERYONE SAYS TOGETHER:
WINE! TRA-LA-LA! HOW DELUXE! HOW CONTINENTAL!

AS A WAY TO RECOGNIZE THE KING- AND QUEENLINESS OF EVERYONE AT THE TABLE, HONOR THE PERSON ON YOUR LEFT BY POURING THEM SOME WINE.

EVERYBODY STAND UP AND SAY THE FOLLOWING BLESSING OVER OUR WINE:

Baruch atah Adonai Eloheinu melech ha'olam, borei pri hagafen.

NOW WE LOOK AT THE SKY, SHUT ONE EYE, AND TOAST SAMMY DAVIS, JR. BY SAYING THE FOLLOWING TOGETHER:

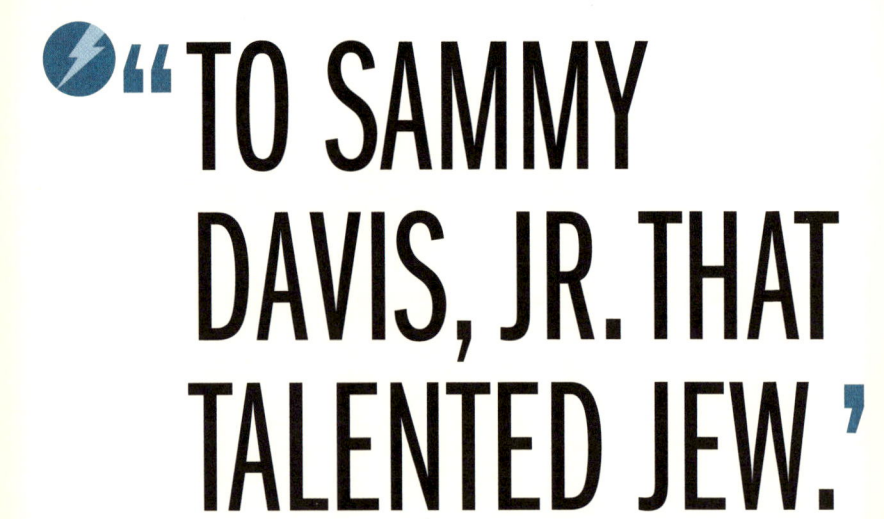

"TO SAMMY DAVIS, JR. THAT TALENTED JEW."

NOW, SIT DOWN AND RECLINE TO THE LEFT AND DRINK SOME WINE AS WE TURN THE PAGE.

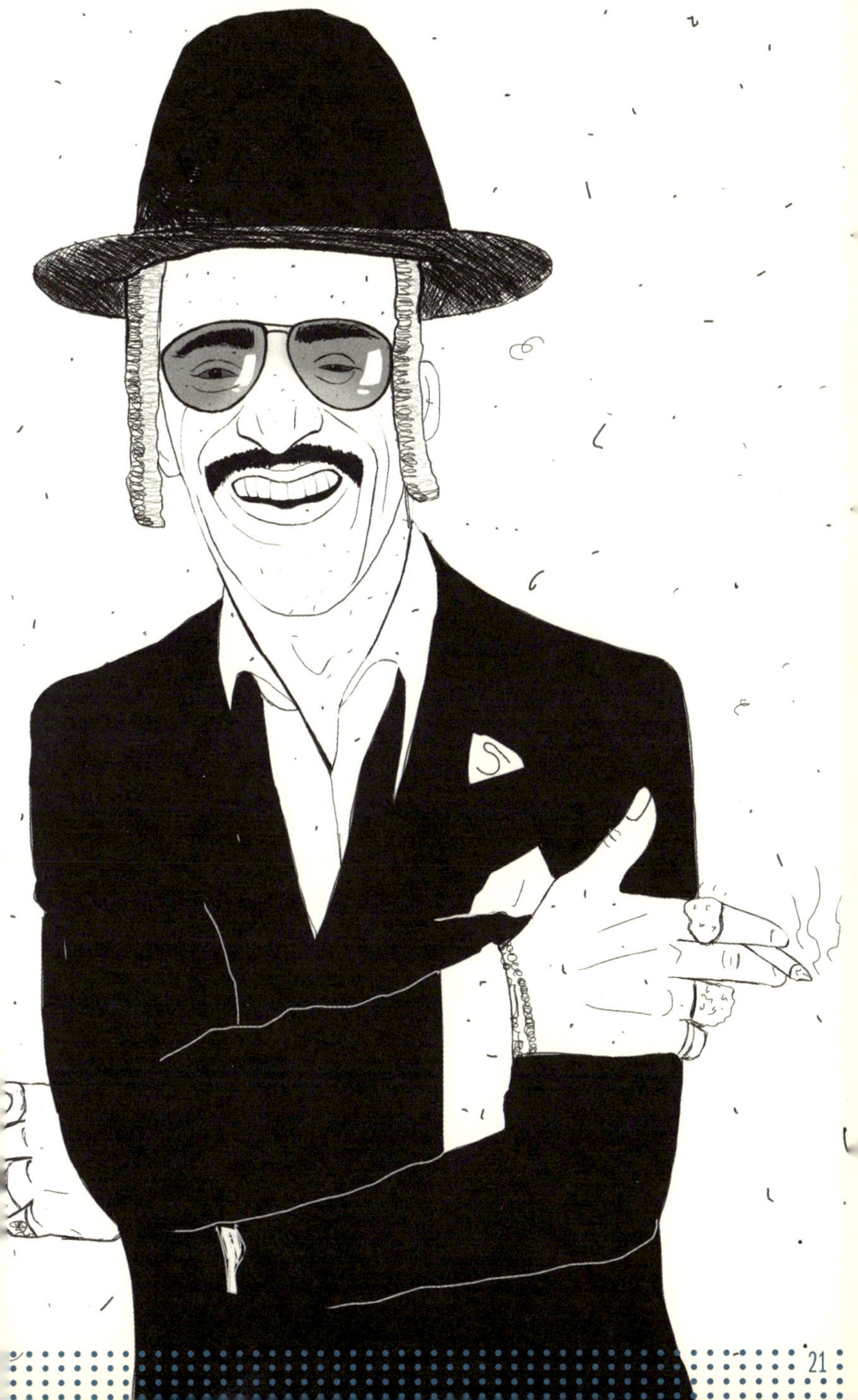

URCHATZ: THE FIRST HAND WASHING / רחץ

In a second, everyone is supposed to wash their hands. Ritual hand washing prepares us for eating with our hands, or performing surgery. It can also be a sign of OCD.

Not to sound neurotic, but did you know that 80 percent of all infectious diseases are passed by human contact?

———————————————

This part of the Seder is when Jesus washed everybody's feet at the Last Supper. Just picture being at dinner with Jesus. All the apostles are there, the table is covered with falafels and hummus and maybe a nice lox. And you get a foot wash. That's a good dinner.

If anyone would like to wash anyone else's feet, do so now. If there are no takers, continue reading.

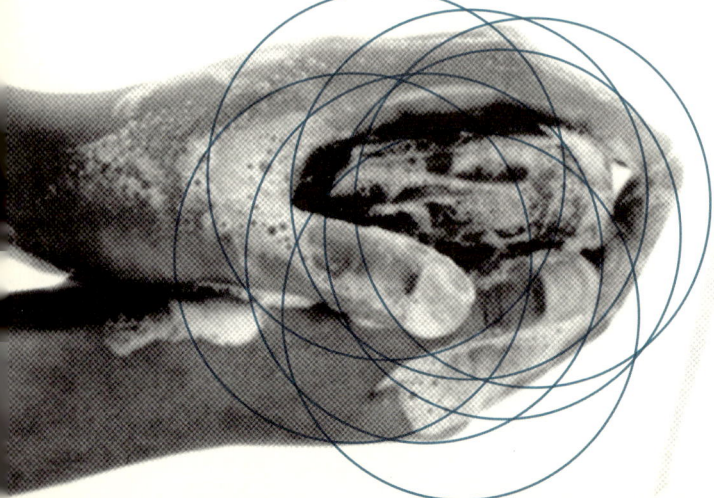

It takes 20 seconds to appropriately wash your hands — getting in between your fingers, getting on top of your knuckles, getting under your nail bed with at least one swoop each time with a lot of soap on, and then rinsing. The Centers for Disease Control recommend singing "Happy Birthday" twice through for an effective wash.
–from "The Secret Life of Germs."

A FUN ACTIVITY PAGE!

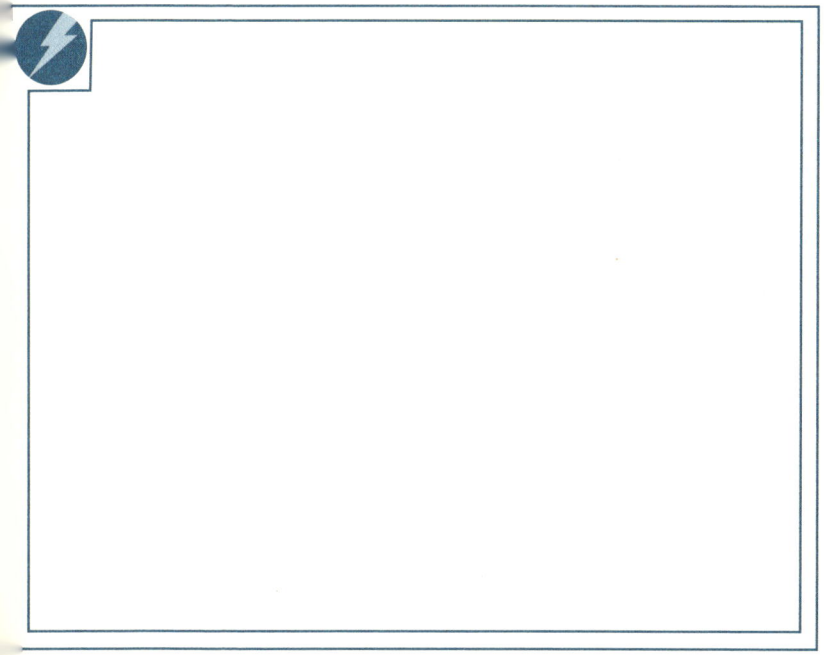

Passover is all about kids. Tonight, we should all have childlike curiosity and ask simple questions. To get us into a childlike state of mind …

Let's do a talent show!

SOMEONE PLEASE STAND AND SHOW OFF A SPECIAL SKILL. A FUNNY ACCENT, POPPING AND LOCKING, WHATEVER YOU GOT. WE'LL WAIT.

MEANWHILE, DRAW A JEW IN THIS BOX.

WHEN THE PERFORMANCE IS DONE, TURN THE PAGE.

25

KARPAS: THE FIRST DIPPING / כרפס

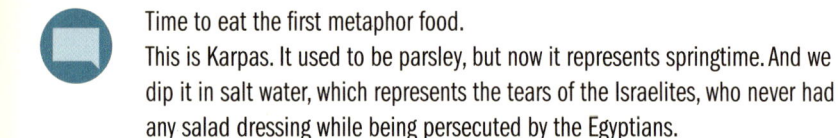

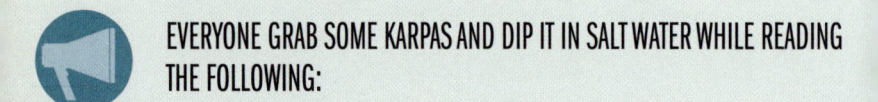

Time to eat the first metaphor food.
This is Karpas. It used to be parsley, but now it represents springtime. And we dip it in salt water, which represents the tears of the Israelites, who never had any salad dressing while being persecuted by the Egyptians.

EVERYONE GRAB SOME KARPAS AND DIP IT IN SALT WATER WHILE READING THE FOLLOWING:

Baruch atah Adonai Eloheinu melech ha'olam, borei pri ha'adama.

What it means: Thank you for making vegetables for us to genetically modify.

YACHATZ: BREAKING THE MATZOH / יחץ

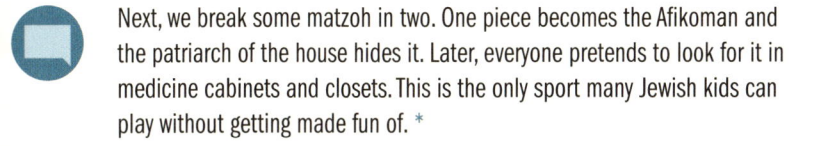

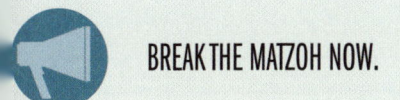

Next, we break some matzoh in two. One piece becomes the Afikoman and the patriarch of the house hides it. Later, everyone pretends to look for it in medicine cabinets and closets. This is the only sport many Jewish kids can play without getting made fun of. *

BREAK THE MATZOH NOW.

If the apartment is too small to hide the Afikoman, the would-be hider may provide a brainteaser to be solved at the end of the meal.

Before we eat this matzoh, let's read this blessing.
Incidentally if we ate this blessing it would taste a lot like matzoh.

EVERYONE READS TOGETHER:

Let all who are hungry, come, and eat.
Let all who are in need, come, and share the Passover meal.
This year we are still here—next year, in the land of Israel or alternate sunny location.
This year we are still slaves—next year, free people (depending how the market goes).

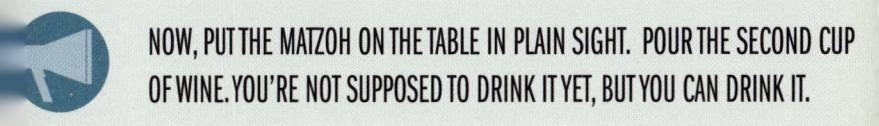

NOW, PUT THE MATZOH ON THE TABLE IN PLAIN SIGHT. POUR THE SECOND CUP OF WINE. YOU'RE NOT SUPPOSED TO DRINK IT YET, BUT YOU CAN DRINK IT.

*THE HOST WILL NOW READ A LIST OF PLACES YOU ARE NOT ALLOWED TO LOOK FOR THE AFIKOMAN.

AT THIS POINT, G
TO ANYBODY YOU

VE A SHOUT-OUT

WISH WAS HERE.

MAGGID: TELLING THE STORY
מגיד

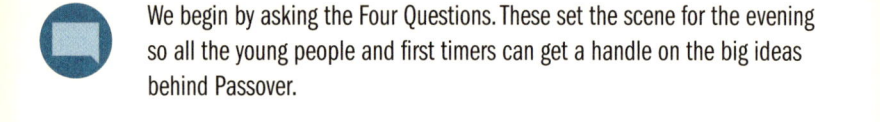

💬 The whole reason we are here is "Maggid," meaning storytelling.

💬 We begin by asking the Four Questions. These set the scene for the evening so all the young people and first timers can get a handle on the big ideas behind Passover.

THE FOUR QUESTIONS/MAH NISHTANAH/מה נשתנה

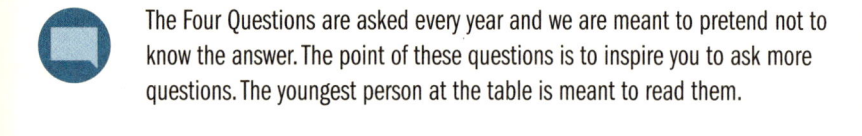

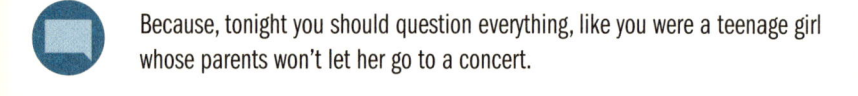

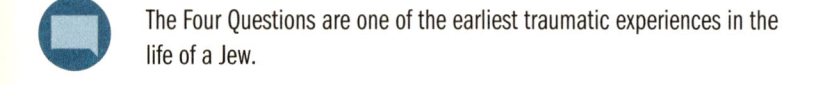

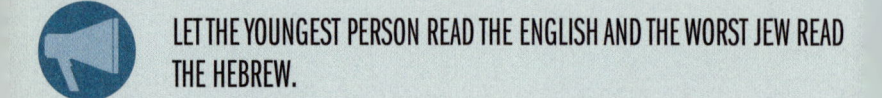

💬 The Four Questions are asked every year and we are meant to pretend not to know the answer. The point of these questions is to inspire you to ask more questions. The youngest person at the table is meant to read them.

💬 Because, tonight you should question everything, like you were a teenage girl whose parents won't let her go to a concert.

💬 The Four Questions are one of the earliest traumatic experiences in the life of a Jew.

📣 **LET THE YOUNGEST PERSON READ THE ENGLISH AND THE WORST JEW READ THE HEBREW.**

מה נשתנה הלילה הזה מכל הלילות?

💬 Mah nishtanah halailah hazeh mikol haleilot?

💬 How is this night different from all other nights?

שבבכל הלילות אנו אוכלין חמץ ומצה הלילה הזה, — כולו מצה!

1.

Sheb'chol haleilot anu ochlin chametz umatzoh, halailah hazeh—kulo matzoh!

On all other nights, we eat whatever kind of bread we like, but why on this night do we eat only matzoh?

EVERYONE READS: Because matzoh is the official food of slaves.

שבכל הלילות אנו אוכלין שאר ירקות, הלילה הזה—מרור!

2.

Sheb'chol haleilot anu ochlin sh'ar y'rakot, halailah hazeh—maror!

On all other nights, we're supposed to eat vegetables, but why on this night do we eat bitter herbs?

EVERYONE READS: Because Jews are bitter.

שֶׁבְּכָל הַלֵּילוֹת אֵין אָנוּ מַטְבִּילִין אֲפִילוּ פַּעַם אֶחָת הַלַּיְלָה הַזֶּה — שְׁתֵּי פְעָמִים!

3.

Sheb'chol haleilot ein anu matbilin afilu pa'am echat, halailah hazeh—sh'tai f'amim!

On all other nights, we don't dip our vegetables even once, but why on this night do we double dip them?

EVERYONE READS: Salt water represents the tears of the Jews, which Egyptians used as a condiment.

שבכל הלילות אנו אוכלין בין יושבין ובין מסבין, הלילה הזה — כלנו מסבין!

4.

Sheb'chol haleilot anu ochlin bein yoshvin uvein m'subin, halailah hazeh—culanu m'subin!

On all other nights, we eat either sitting upright or reclining, but why on this night do we all recline?

EVERYONE READS: Because we have to be comfortable tonight. So, get comfortable. Get real comfortable. No farting.

NOW, THE YOUNGEST PERSON MAY SELECT A FIFTH QUESTION FOR THE OLDEST TO ANSWER FROM THIS LIST:

- How long could you handle solitary confinement?
- If there was a god, what would he love most about you?
- Have you ever spoken to yourself out loud into a mirror and what did you say?
- Which rapper are you most like and why?
- Who do you look up to most at the table?
- In a post-apocalyptic scenario, what outfit would you wear and where would you live?
- What's your favorite movie quote and why?
- What are some good things to remember in an emergency?

IT'S TIME TO TELL THE EXODUS STORY.

DO "THE WAVE" THREE TIMES, STARTING WITH THE READER AND MOVING CLOCKWISE.

This story has been retold over and over again to remind us not to get too comfortable in our lives. People still think Jews run the banks, and there's always some nut who wants to eradicate the nerds in charge of the money.

And remember that this story is one of many. Right this second there are people all over the world running for their lives. Tonight, we should think of them and tell their stories. Tomorrow, we should find out how we can help.

It's important to take a moment and address a big question about this Exodus story. Jewish slaves built the pyramids, right? But, what about all the people that say no human could have done that?

What about the aliens? Where do they fit in?

If the Jews were working for Pharaoh, whom was Pharaoh working for? Evidence suggests the Egyptians were actually working for beings from another galaxy.

You be the judge.

HERE'S SOME PROOF I FOUND ON THE INTERNET THAT ALIENS BUILT THE PYRAMIDS:

If you take the perimeter of the pyramid and divide it by two times the height, you get exactly the number pi (3.14159…) up to the fifteenth digit. However, pi was not calculated accurately to the fourth digit until the 6th century.

The sides of the base of the pyramid are some 757 feet long, with a difference in length of about two centimeters and they were made before Home Depot.

The Egyptians kept very careful records about everything they ever did: every king they had, every war they fought, and every structure they built. There were no records of them ever having built the pyramids. Very Watergatey.

The bricks that built the pyramids weigh about two tons each. But, the Egyptians hadn't yet invented the wheel when they were made. Or the elevator.

King Tut's tomb was filled with fungus never before seen on earth. So, his cleaning lady certainly didn't build the pyramids.

SOURCE: HTTP://WWW.ALIEN-UFOS.COM

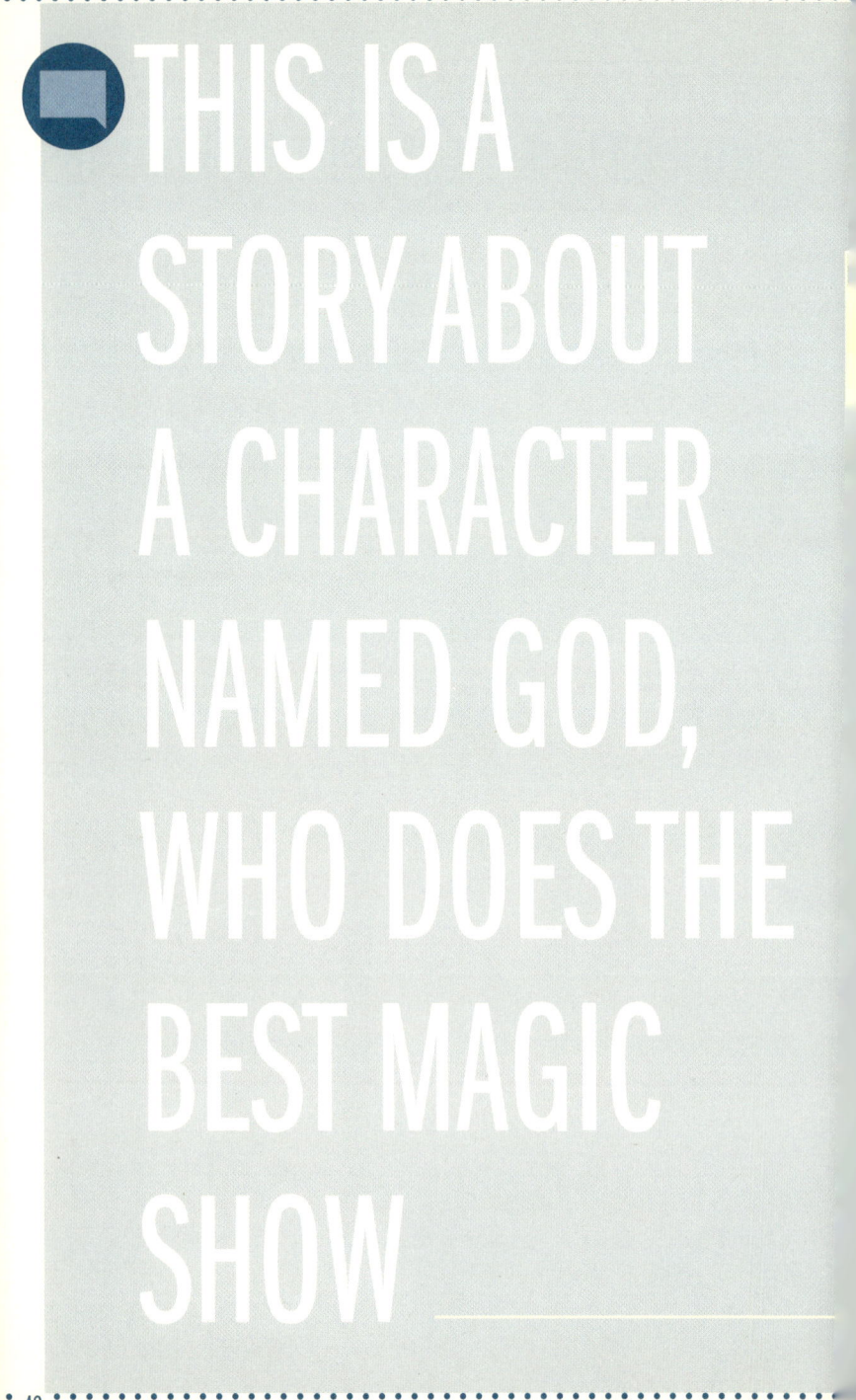

THIS IS A STORY ABOUT A CHARACTER NAMED GOD, WHO DOES THE BEST MAGIC SHOW

EVER TO CONVINCE A GUY WITH A SEVERE SPEECH IMPEDIMENT TO SAVE THE WORLD

📢 **(EVERYONE CLEAR YOUR THROAT.)**

💬 **(CONTINUE TO ALTERNATE READERS.)**

Once upon a time, way pre-Jesus, a Pharaoh in Egypt decided there were way too many Jews.

Throughout history, this has been a remarkably common perception.

As a way to control the Jewish population, the Pharaoh at the time decreed that all male newborns (or Jewborns) be thrown in the Nile. As you've no doubt heard, Jews are not great swimmers, especially as babies.

Our story begins when right in the middle of this baby-throwing debacle, a scrappy little Israelite named Moses was born. He was one of those babies that looks like a weird old man, but he's still cute, because he's a baby.

He was so cute in fact, that rather than drown him, his Mom put him in a little baby boat and placed him on the Nile in hopes he'd float to Miami. He never made it there, but her small act of bravery pretty much saved the Jews, and, as a side note, led to the ritual circumcision of billions of men.

📢 **ANYONE WHO WISHES THEY STILL HAD A FORESKIN RAISE YOUR HAND.**

Moses floated down the river in his little boat, which would have made an awesome YouTube video. He washed up onshore and was found by none other than the Pharaoh's daughter, who wanted to keep him, because he was a cute little Jew baby who looked like a weird old man.

Fast forward a couple of decades.

The Pharaoh's daughter raised Moses and he grew up in high society. He spent all day eating hummus and baklava while drawing hieroglyphics.

But then, one day Moses was on a jog along the Nile, no doubt listening to an iPod provided by the alien overlords no one seems to want to talk about. It was a lovely Egyptian day at a balmy 135 degrees, and he smiled at everyone he passed.

He was resting at a water fountain shaped like the head of Osiris, when he saw an Egyptian beating up an Israelite on the street. Rather than try to reason with the bully, he walked right over and beat up the Egyptian. To death. He knew immediately he had to leave Egypt or he was gonna be in big, big trouble. So, as was the style of the time, he decided to go into exile.

Moses ran for the hills and went deep, deep undercover.

MAKE A MUSTACHE WITH YOUR FINGER AND SEE IF ANYONE CAN FIND YOU.

Let's stop for a moment, to talk about Moses.

Exile is hard. Many of us have been exiled to the couch, but few of us have ever been asked to go sleep on the couch in another country. The challenges of an exile are endless. From figuring out how to date in a new city, to finding new favorite restaurants, an exile is truly starting over.

This was especially true of Moses. He was good-looking, but he had some issues, which would have made it hard for him to fit in. According to legend he had a major speech impediment. Some say he had a stutter, which is not a big deal, unless you speak Hebrew, a language made primarily of spitting sounds and yelling at people. But, some say his impediment was much, much worse.

There is a story that tells of a time when Moses was a baby. The Pharaoh loved hanging out with him. But, whenever he was near, Moses would always try to grab the Pharaoh's crown and put it on his own head. Pharaoh's advisers, who had obviously never, ever seen a baby do anything, didn't understand that this was because babies try to put everything in their mouth or throw it at the dog. Pharaoh's advisers (most likely aliens) decided that Baby Moses's behavior was a sign that he would one day grow up and usurp the crown.

That's a lotta pressure for a baby.

So, they devised a test in which Moses would be placed in front of the gold crown and a plate of bright and shiny burning coals. If he reached for the crown, it meant he was intelligent and should be executed. If he reached for the coals I guess it meant that he was an idiot and they should feel sorry for him.

Being a good Jewish boy, Moses reached for the crown. But, the angel Gabriel, who is often depicted playing a trumpet with his penis exposed, reached down from heaven and moved Moses's hand toward the coal. We can assume Gabriel was invisible at the time, which explains why he's always depicted playing trumpet with his penis exposed.

Moses took the coal and put it in his mouth because babies are totally stupid sometimes. Then, he probably threw it at the dog.

But, most importantly for our story, he gave himself a lifelong speech impediment.

NOW BACK TO THE EXODUS.

Years after Moses skedaddled, life in Egypt really sucked for the Jews. There were no good delis in town and they were forced to carry huge sandstone bricks 14 hours a day to make gigantic cat statues designed by the alien overlords.

At this point, God speaks to Moses. We're not sure how, this was before the Internet.

RAISE YOUR HAND IF YOU'VE EVER SPOKEN TO OR BEEN SPOKEN TO BY GOD.

God told Moses to get back to Egypt and save the Jews. Moses didn't think he could do it, so he told God no. So, God appeared as a Burning Bush.

Moses still didn't think he could do it, and he told God no again. So, God turned a rod into a snake and a leprous hand into a normal hand and then he turned a normal river into a river of blood.

A F*#%ING RIVER OF BLOOD.

That's why he's God and you work in retail or whatever.

Moses grew a pair and decided he could do it. He went back to Egypt and told the Pharaoh that if he didn't let the Jews stop making cat statues, then God would be very, very upset with him.

But, Pharaoh assumed the Hebrews were just trying to slack off, so he didn't heed the warning.

So, God sent ten plagues to Egypt and things got biblical.

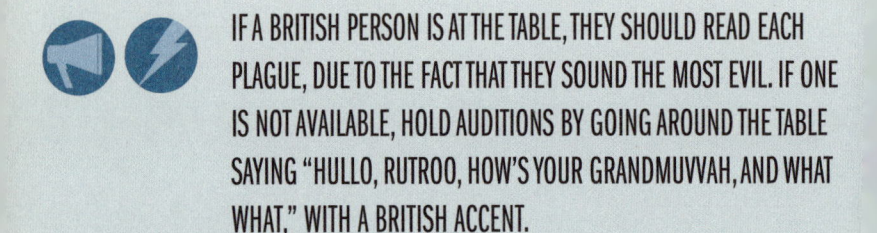

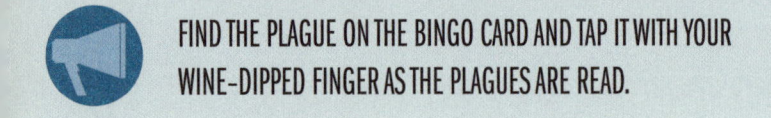

The Holy One Blessed Be He brought ten plagues on the Egyptians in Egypt. These are the ten:

alivi 'eshr makivt shbya haqaidevsh bairevik, hevia 'eal ha'mitesryem bimitsrayim valevi hn:

Now, tradition dictates that at this point we recite the plagues and dip a finger in the wine, removing a drop for each plague as it is said.

Instead let's play Plague Bingo.

IF A BRITISH PERSON IS AT THE TABLE, THEY SHOULD READ EACH PLAGUE, DUE TO THE FACT THAT THEY SOUND THE MOST EVIL. IF ONE IS NOT AVAILABLE, HOLD AUDITIONS BY GOING AROUND THE TABLE SAYING "HULLO, RUTROO, HOW'S YOUR GRANDMUVVAH, AND WHAT WHAT," WITH A BRITISH ACCENT.

FIND THE PLAGUE ON THE BINGO CARD AND TAP IT WITH YOUR WINE-DIPPED FINGER AS THE PLAGUES ARE READ.

BLOOD · FROGS · LICE · SWARMS OF INSECTS · CATTLE DISEASE · BOILS · HAIL · LOCUSTS · DARKNESS · DEATH OF THE FIRSTBORN

10

B I N G O

LOCUSTS	PARTY POOPERS	BOILS	BAD ACID	FROGS
WEAK WIFI SIGNAL	BLOOD	SHRINKAGE	DEATH OF FIRSTBORN	ZOMBIES
CATTLE DISEASE	FREE HUGS	FREE	PLAQUE	HAIL
BELIEBERS	LICE	CHICKEN POX	CANKLES	HALITOSIS
DARKNESS	ADULT ACNE	FARTS	JIMMY LEGS	SWARM OF INSECTS

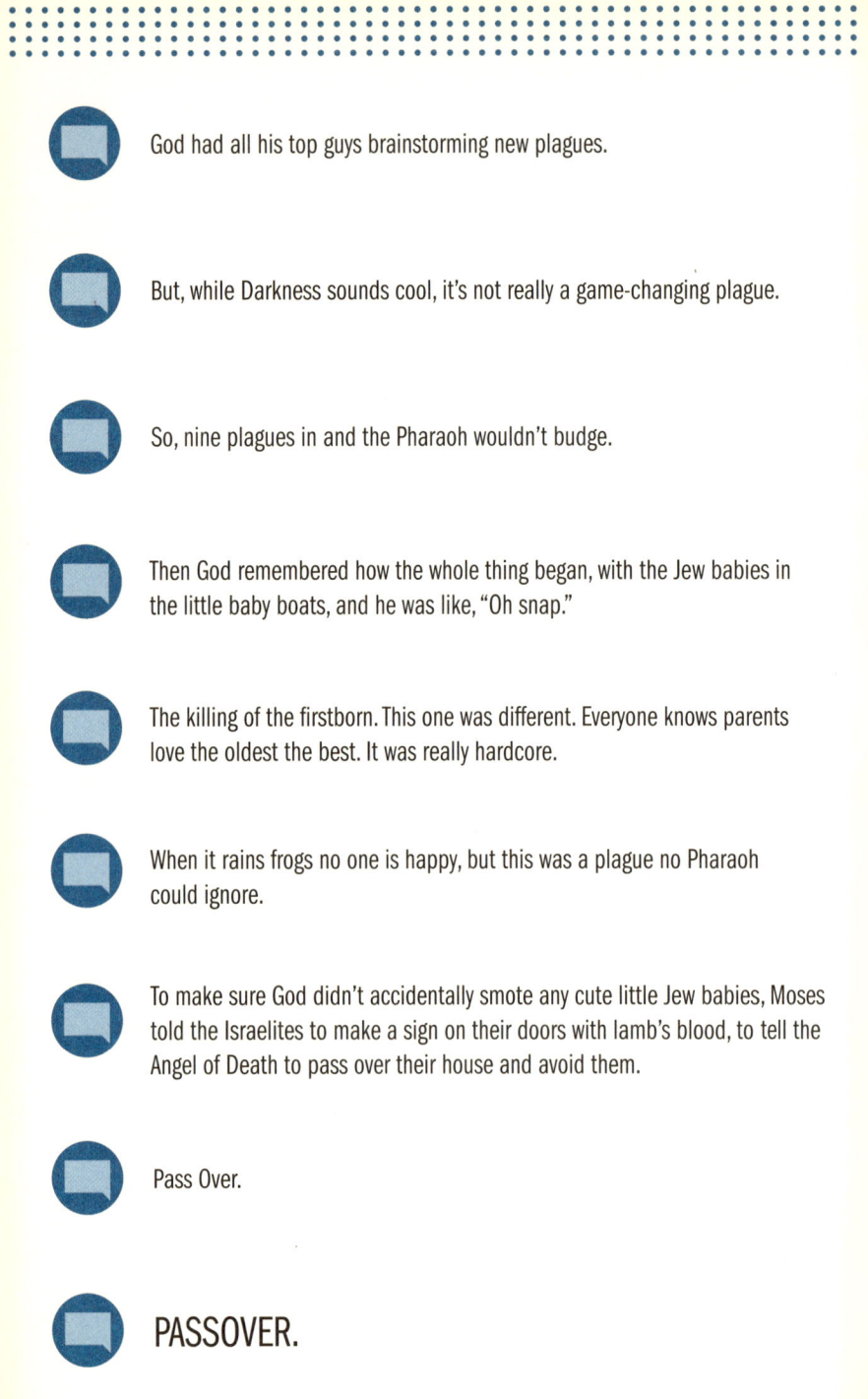

- God had all his top guys brainstorming new plagues.

- But, while Darkness sounds cool, it's not really a game-changing plague.

- So, nine plagues in and the Pharaoh wouldn't budge.

- Then God remembered how the whole thing began, with the Jew babies in the little baby boats, and he was like, "Oh snap."

- The killing of the firstborn. This one was different. Everyone knows parents love the oldest the best. It was really hardcore.

- When it rains frogs no one is happy, but this was a plague no Pharaoh could ignore.

- To make sure God didn't accidentally smote any cute little Jew babies, Moses told the Israelites to make a sign on their doors with lamb's blood, to tell the Angel of Death to pass over their house and avoid them.

- Pass Over.

- **PASSOVER.**

Incidentally, no one ever really talks about the lambs.

READ THIS SHORT STORY AS IF YOU WERE IN A CLASSROOM FULL OF CHILDREN.

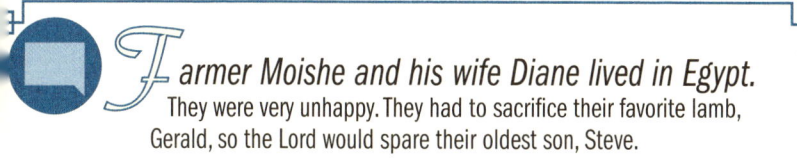

Farmer Moishe and his wife Diane lived in Egypt.
They were very unhappy. They had to sacrifice their favorite lamb, Gerald, so the Lord would spare their oldest son, Steve.

All the animals were confused.

"What does a lamb have to do with anything?" asked Myrtle the cow.

"They always go for the nice guys first," said Mayor Tartington, who was a hog.

Gerald ate some grass to clear his head and tried to nap.
But, Tim, the chicken, wouldn't leave him alone.

"Gerald!" he squawked. "Gerald! Can I have your stereo?"

At that very moment, Farmer Moishe came out of the house with a shiny ax.
He slapped a few locusts away from his face and looked for Gerald.

"C'mere, Gerald," he called. You could tell he'd been crying.

Storm clouds as thick as schmaltz covered the moon, as Gerald took his last breath of fresh farm air.

- So, the Pharaoh was having the shittiest week of his life. He had lice, his cows wouldn't stop puking, and all the boys in his oldest kid's school simultaneously perished.

- He told the Jews that they were all evicted from their condos and their deposits would not be refunded.

- All the Jews had heard they would be leaving Egypt, so everybody was busy packing. It was mostly just loincloths. But, they needed food for the trip and that night everybody was baking bread for sandwiches.

- The news that the Pharaoh had freed them spread fast and they didn't waste time. They didn't even wait for the bread to rise; they threw the dry crispy crackers in a box and called it matzoh.

- Tonight, we eat matzoh to commemorate that night. It's not very good, but that's the point. It's hard to think about suffering with a mouthful of blueberry pie.

- We'll also get a chance to enjoy matzoh ball soup, which certainly is delicious. Incidentally, each matzoh ball expands to three times its original size when consumed, so eat with caution.

After the reading of the Exodus story, someone traditionally says "speaking of great stories" and launches into an anecdote that has no place at the dinner table.

This is often the best part of the night.

AT THIS POINT ONE PERSON SHOULD VOLUNTEER TO TELL A SHORT AND WILDLY INAPPROPRIATE STORY.

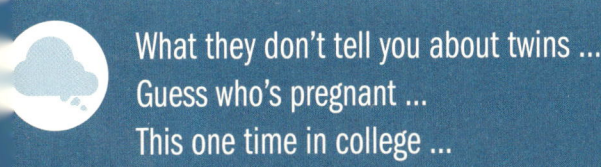

Here are some thought starters to get you going:

What they don't tell you about twins ...
Guess who's pregnant ...
This one time in college ...
This dinner reminds me of how much I enjoy lovemaking in groups ...
I met some of my best friends in prison ...
I dated this one dude who was a real freak in the sack ...
Look at these photos on my phone, I think they might be illegal ...
Here's a funny story from AA ...
Did I ever tell about the time Great-Grandpa was bisexual?
Let me tell something you didn't know about the art of drug-muling ...

THE SECOND CUP: REDEMPTION / כוס שני

Now, we toast the Israelites for rolling out of Egypt in time and generally being clever with our second cup of wine.

Here's a list of things they've invented since 1901:

Jeans, Lipstick, Hollywood, the Fax Machine, the Ballpoint Pen, Woodstock, Contraceptives, Instant Coffee, the Theory of Relativity, Television Remote Control, Psychoanalysis, and the Weekend.

The Blimp, Pawn Shops, Videotape, Color Television, Traffic Lights, the Microphone, Scotchguard, Cheesecake, Cafeterias, Chemotherapy, Stand-up Comedy, and the Flexistraw.

The Atomic Bomb, Discount Stores, Lasers, Google, Instant Photography, the Walkie-Talkie, the Thermonuclear Bomb, and Tapered Roller Bearings.

Genetic Engineering, the Nuclear Chain Reactor, the Ready-to-Wear Clothing Industry, Virtual Reality, Def Jam Records, Capitalism, Holograms, and Prozac.

Jews currently make up approximately 0.25 percent of the world's population and 2 percent of the U.S. population.

They also comprise 23 percent of all Nobel Prize winners and 37 percent of the U.S. Nobel Prize winners.

Baruch atah Adonai ga'al Yisrael.
Baruch atah Adonai Eloheinu melech ha'olam, borei pri hagafen.

Thanks for getting us out of Egypt before the situation got cray-cray.

DRINK THE SECOND CUP OF WINE WHILE LEANING TO THE LEFT.

DAYENU / דייֵנוּ·

Dayenu is the best Jewish song that isn't by Barbra Streisand.

It's totally catchy with a chorus everyone can sing along to. In Afghanistan and Iran they like to hit each other over the head with green onions while they sing it, as a way to train them not to ever yearn to return to Egypt.

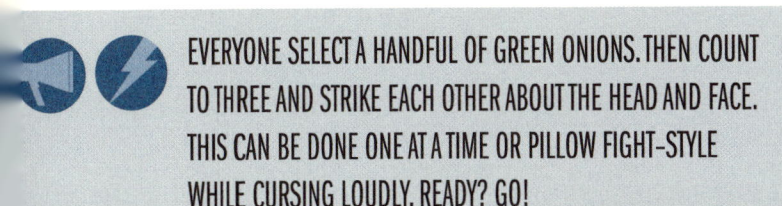

EVERYONE SELECT A HANDFUL OF GREEN ONIONS. THEN COUNT TO THREE AND STRIKE EACH OTHER ABOUT THE HEAD AND FACE. THIS CAN BE DONE ONE AT A TIME OR PILLOW FIGHT-STYLE WHILE CURSING LOUDLY. READY? GO!

THE SEDER PLATE

Now, one last thing before the actual eating begins. Please direct your attention to the round plate with stuff on it. This is called the Seder Plate on which there are six symbolic foods and some extras:

THE SHANK / זרוֹעַ

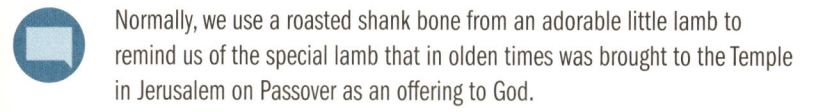

Normally, we use a roasted shank bone from an adorable little lamb to remind us of the special lamb that in olden times was brought to the Temple in Jerusalem on Passover as an offering to God.

It's hard to find a good shank in these parts, so, tonight we use an improvised blade called a shank, to remind us that there are almost eight million Americans in jail or on parole, more than half are Black and Latino, and God doesn't seem to be raining frogs on their behalf.

THE EGG / ביצה

A boiled or roasted egg is smooth and round and symbolizes the new life that comes with springtime.

Tonight we decorate the egg like an Easter egg because why should the Goys have all the fun?!

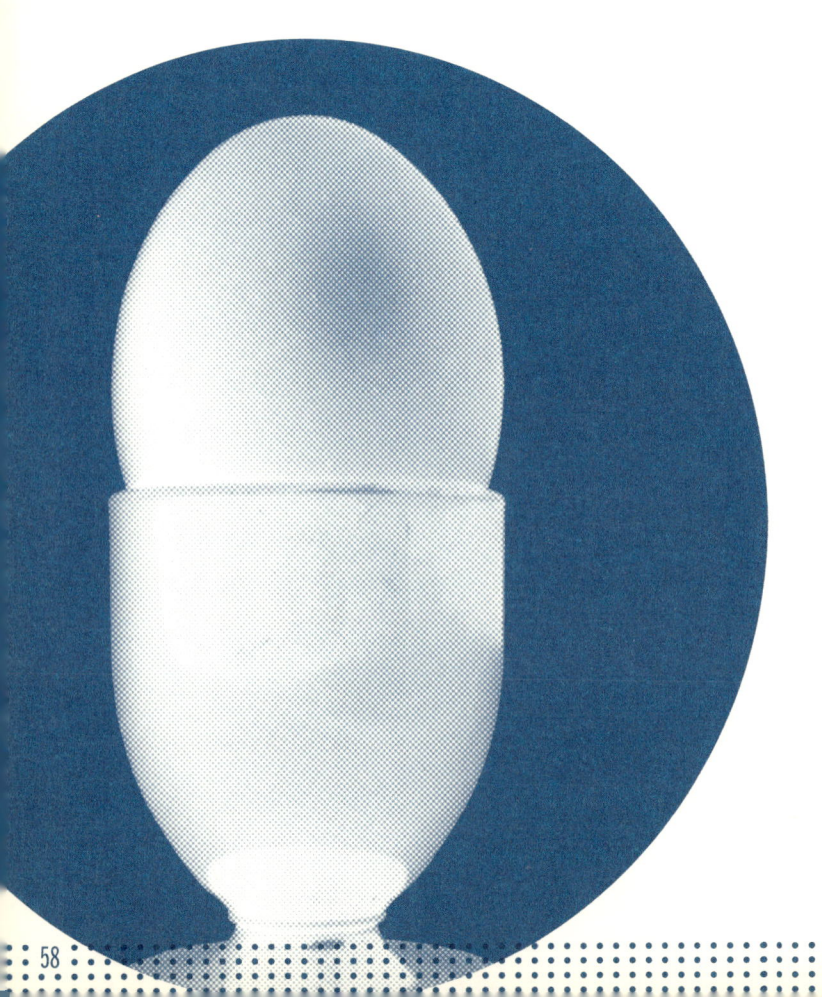

MAROR / מרור

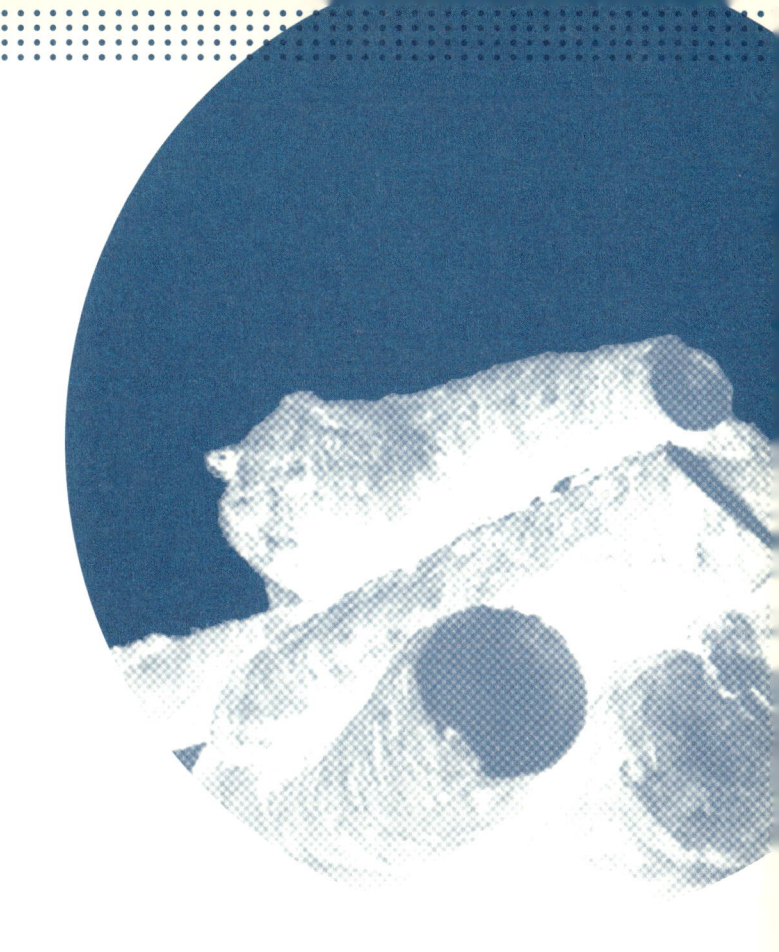

A bitter herb, in this case horseradish, reminds us of the bitterness of Egyptian bondage.

We eat horseradish because no one makes a slavery-flavored ice cream.

KARPAS / כרפס

A green vegetable reminds us that Passover occurs during springtime when new life brings a feeling of hope.

Not to mention capri pants.

CHAROSET / חרוסת

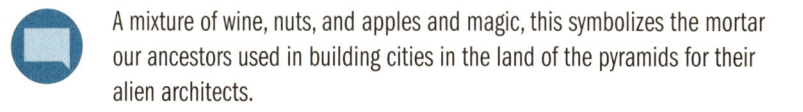

A mixture of wine, nuts, and apples and magic, this symbolizes the mortar our ancestors used in building cities in the land of the pyramids for their alien architects.

This is also what ancient Jews used instead of Legos.

THE SEDER PLATE EXTRAS!!

THE ORANGE / תפוז

A modern addition to the Seder Plate. When women were first becoming rabbis, a lady named Susannah Heschel was traveling in Florida, the Land of Oranges. One night she spoke at a synagogue about the emerging equality of women in Jewish life. After she spoke, a fat annoying man stood up and said in the nasal voice of a dick, "A woman belongs on the bimah as much as an orange belongs on the seder plate!"

Ever since that day, we place an orange on the Seder Plate, as a big "f you" to haters everywhere. Tonight, we use a gay orange as a way to remember that absolutely everybody should have a place at the table.

The Equal Rights Amendment (ERA) guaranteeing rights to women in America was written by Alice Paul and, in 1923, it was introduced in Congress for the first time. After a few subsequent attempts, it has failed to pass in every session since 1982.

Barring gay marriage was declared unconstitutional in 1993, but as of this writing the battle continues.

ESEV UGIYAH / עשבים עוגיות

Weed macaroons. Include these as a way to remember that spirituality and rebellion go hand in hand.

It seems obvious that if there is a God, he's high most of the time.

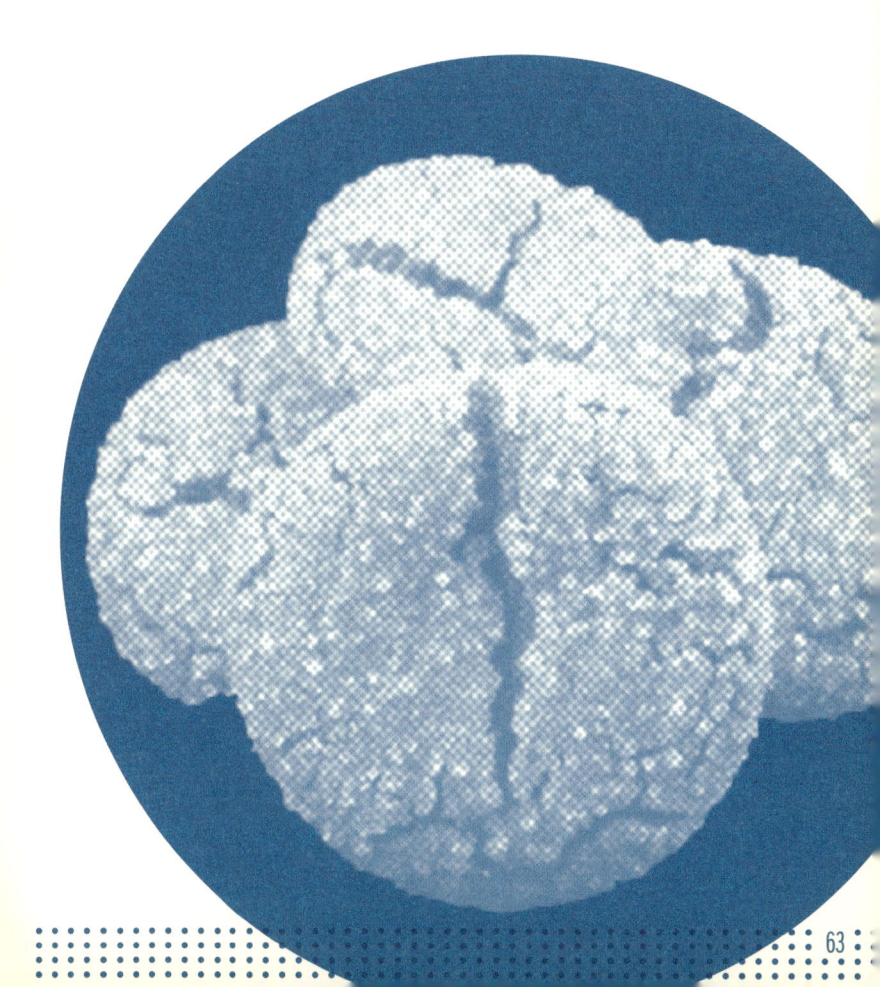

MOTZI MATZOH: EATING THE MATZOH / מוציא מצה

This is the one time during Passover in which one is obligated to eat matzoh. It has to be the plain kind, none of your fancy pants flavored nonsense.

THE LEADER OF YOUR DINNER HOLDS THREE PIECES OF MATZOH, WITH THE MIDDLE PIECE BROKEN. THEN, HE/SHE SAYS THE FOLLOWING TWO PRAYERS, NEITHER OF WHICH MAKE MUCH SENSE:

Baruch atah Adonai Eloheinu melech ha'olam, hamotzi lechem min ha'aretz.

Baruch atah Adonai Eloheinu melech ha'olam, asher kideshanu b'mitzvotav, v'tzivanu al achilat matzoh.

What it means: Thank you for making us eat matzoh.
Yeah. Thanks a lot.

MAROR: BITTER HERB / מרור

> NOW, WE TAKE SOME MAROR AND DIP IT IN CHAROSET. DON'T USE MATZOH.

> RECITE THE BLESSING AND EAT, BUT FOR CHRIST'S SAKE DO NOT RECLINE.

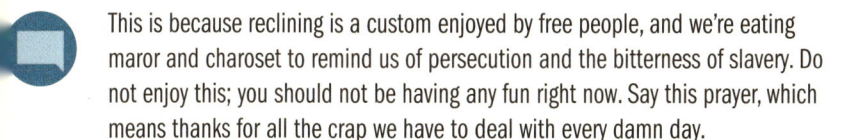

This is because reclining is a custom enjoyed by free people, and we're eating maror and charoset to remind us of persecution and the bitterness of slavery. Do not enjoy this; you should not be having any fun right now. Say this prayer, which means thanks for all the crap we have to deal with every damn day.

Baruch atah Adonai Eloheinu melech ha'olam, asher kideshanu b'mitzvotav, v'tzivanu al achilat maror.

KORECH: HILLEL'S SANDWICH / כורך

Now for the final pre-dinner metaphor dining experience.

We have just eaten maror without matzoh, which sucked. But, in the days of the Temple, i.e., "The Good Ol' Days," Hillel, AKA the Jewish Dagwood, who was the head of the Sanhedrin, AKA the Jewish Ninjas, used to make them into a sandwich with Passover lamb, matzoh, and maror.

Eating Hillel's famous sandwich tonight reminds us of the way life combines moments of suffering (maror) with relief (matzoh).

Other ways we could do this are by skateboarding on a busy highway, snorting Kool-Aid mix, or bag-tagging ourselves while getting a foot massage.

Make Hillel's Sandwich, AKA Jew S'Mores, AKA The Freedomwich, and eat it while reclining to the left.

SHULCHAN ORECH: THE PASSOVER MEAL IS SERVED
שלחן עורך

DINNER TIME BONUS CONVERSATION!!

Every Passover we tell the story of the Four Sons at a Seder, who represent the four types of people you encounter at dinner parties.

The Wise Son, who asks *"What are the testimonials, statutes, and laws God commanded you and will there be a quiz?"*

The Wicked Son asks *"This sucks. Why can't I just party all night long?"*

The Simple Son, who asks *"Wha? Huh? Who brung dat?"*

And the Son Who Does Not Know How to Ask doesn't say anything.

In modern society, we are all Wise Sons because we have Google and TV and educations. But, when we do so much listening and learning to a constant flow of information, it's easy to become the Son Who Doesn't Know How to Ask. So, tonight, we choose a Wicked Son. Who was the most evil person of last year and why? Discuss as you enjoy your meal.

EAT!

KOSHER/NOT KOSHER

Here's a fun game to entertain the kids while the food comes out. It's called Kosher/Not Kosher and the rules are simple. Pick an edible substance from the list. If you guess right, you go to heaven. If you guess wrong you'll be doomed to walk the Hall of Souls for all eternity. Fun!

A. PASTE

B. A PIG

C. A POLICE OFFICER

D. TOAST

E. A CELEBRITY

F. A RACCOON

G. AN ELEPHANT

H. JEFFERSON AIRPLANE

I. A FRISBEE

J. YOUR OWN HAND

K. A SHOE

L. A REALLY GOOD SHOW

M. A PIMPLE	**N.** TALCUM POWDER	**O.** A SHIM	**P.** HUMAN SKIN
Q. A CAN	**R.** A SNAKE	**S.** THE BAND WHITESNAKE	**T.** STEVE URKEL
U. HOUSE MUSIC	**V.** LIBERACE	**W.** 2014 KIA SEDONA	**X.** PALLBEARERS
Y. PAUL REUBENS	**Z.** REUBENS		

NOW, PUT THIS THING AWAY AND EAT SOME DINNER!

ANSWERS:
KOSHER: A, I, N, O, U, W · MAYBE: D, K, L, M, Q

TZAFUN: THE AFIKOMAN / צפון

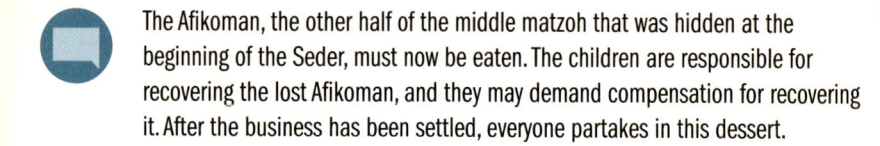

The Afikoman, the other half of the middle matzoh that was hidden at the beginning of the Seder, must now be eaten. The children are responsible for recovering the lost Afikoman, and they may demand compensation for recovering it. After the business has been settled, everyone partakes in this dessert.

If you are instead doing a brainteaser, the solver gets first dibs on the weed cookies.

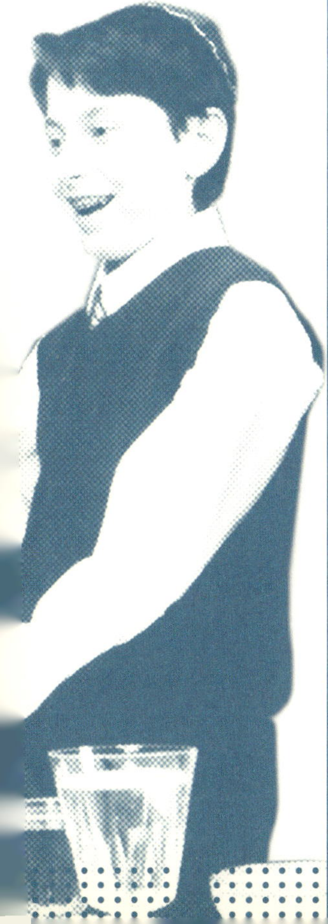

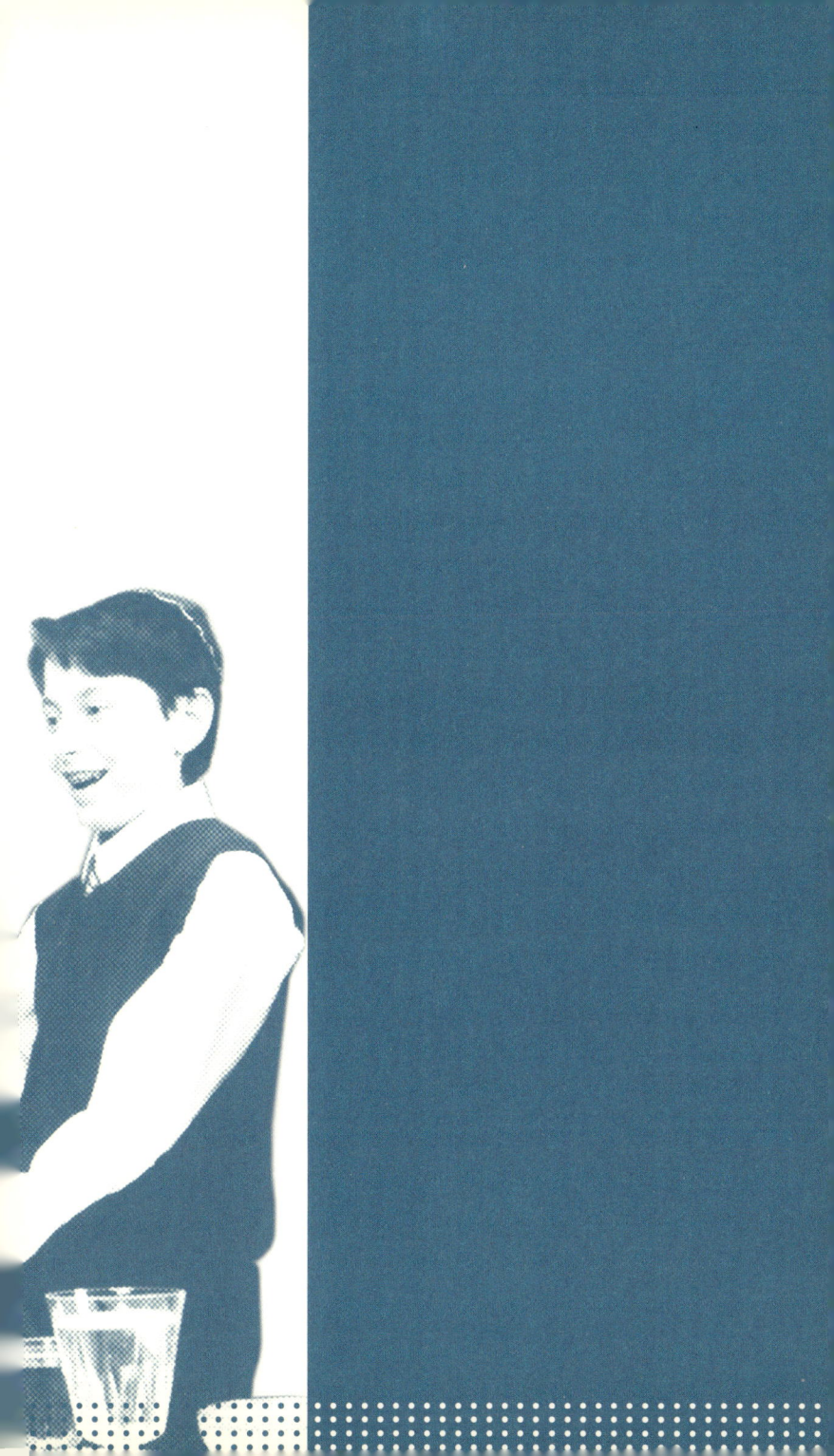

THE STORY OF ELIJAH

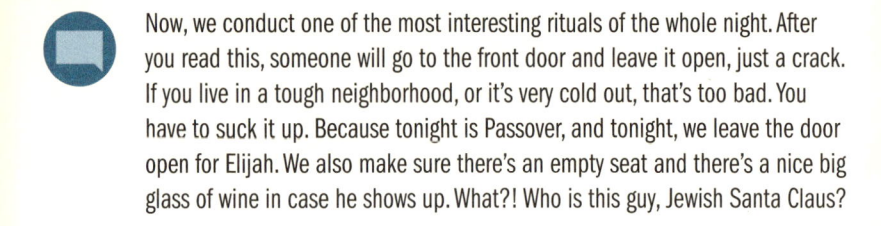

Now, we conduct one of the most interesting rituals of the whole night. After you read this, someone will go to the front door and leave it open, just a crack. If you live in a tough neighborhood, or it's very cold out, that's too bad. You have to suck it up. Because tonight is Passover, and tonight, we leave the door open for Elijah. We also make sure there's an empty seat and there's a nice big glass of wine in case he shows up. What?! Who is this guy, Jewish Santa Claus?

No. He's the Easter Bunny meets the Grim Reaper meets a Jehovah's Witness out for revenge.

In the Bible (another book written by Jews) Elijah is the one character who doesn't die. So, what happens to him? Some Bible stuff, that's what. One day, he's out prophesizing and a chariot, which is being pulled by enormous horses who happen to be ON FIRE, lands on earth, picks him up, and flies him to outer space.

That's so metal. What's even more metal is that he's coming back. Tonight. Through your front door.

He's going to walk in, pound a glass of Manischewitz, sit down for a sec, and announce the Messiah's impending arrival.

Then, the next day the dead arise from their graves, the Messiah shows up, and the world as we know it is over. This is the type of stuff people come up with when you oppress them for thousands of years.

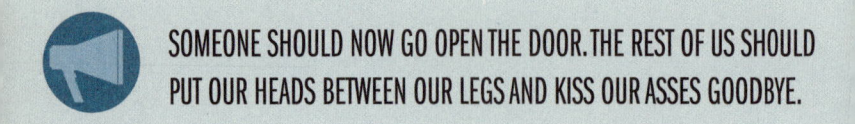

SOMEONE SHOULD NOW GO OPEN THE DOOR. THE REST OF US SHOULD PUT OUR HEADS BETWEEN OUR LEGS AND KISS OUR ASSES GOODBYE.

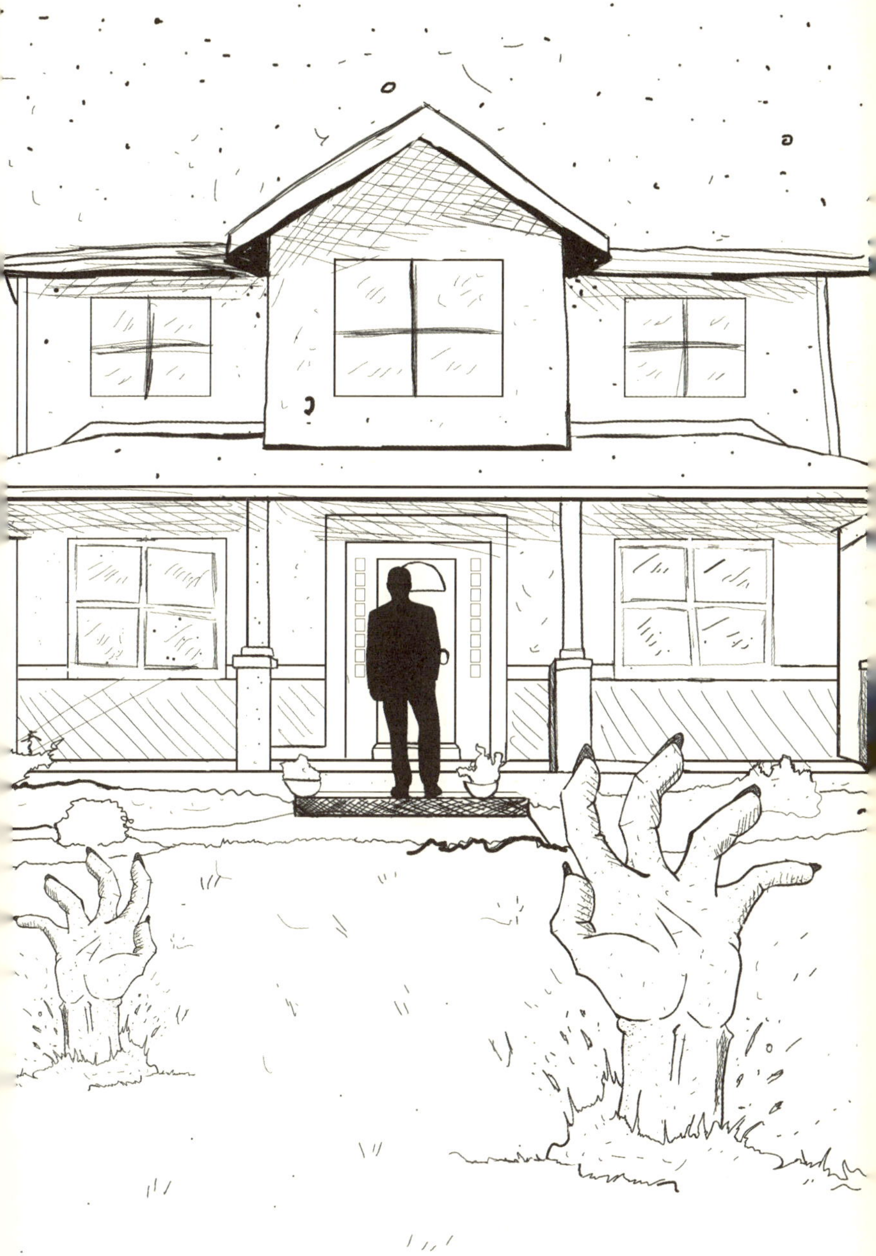

HALLEL: PSALMS OF PRAISE

Now, we will sing the greatest song ever about spiritual enlightenment and the human journey.

PLAY THE KARAOKE VERSION OF "I BELIEVE I CAN FLY" BY R. KELLY OFF OF A COMPUTER AND SING ALONG. THIS IS THE CHORUS, FULL LYRICS AVAILABLE ONLINE.

YOU SHOULD DRINK THE LAST TWO GLASSES OF WINE WHILE YOU SING.

SING IT LIKE YOU MEAN IT.

I believe I can fly
I believe I can touch the sky
I think about it every night and day
Spread my wings and fly away
I believe I can soar
I see me running through that open door
I believe I can fly...

75

FOR THE BRAVE HOST

THE SEDER PLATE FOR *THE UNORTHODOX HAGGADAH* REQUIRES JUST A FEW SPECIAL PREPARATIONS

THE SHANK
Rather than use the traditional shank bone, we use a shank, or improvised prison weapon. Below find simple instructions or design your own. Have fun!
1. First, get a piece of paper (any kind of paper will work but printer paper and card stock work best) and cut a length you want your shank to be.
2. Next, roll the paper up the the width of a thumbtack.
3. Tape the paper.
4. Push a thumbtack into the paper roll until the point is only visible. You're shwelcome!

THE EGG
Rather than a plain old hard-boiled egg, we suggest an Easter egg. The more religious icons you can squeeze on the better. Or, just decorate it with a marker.

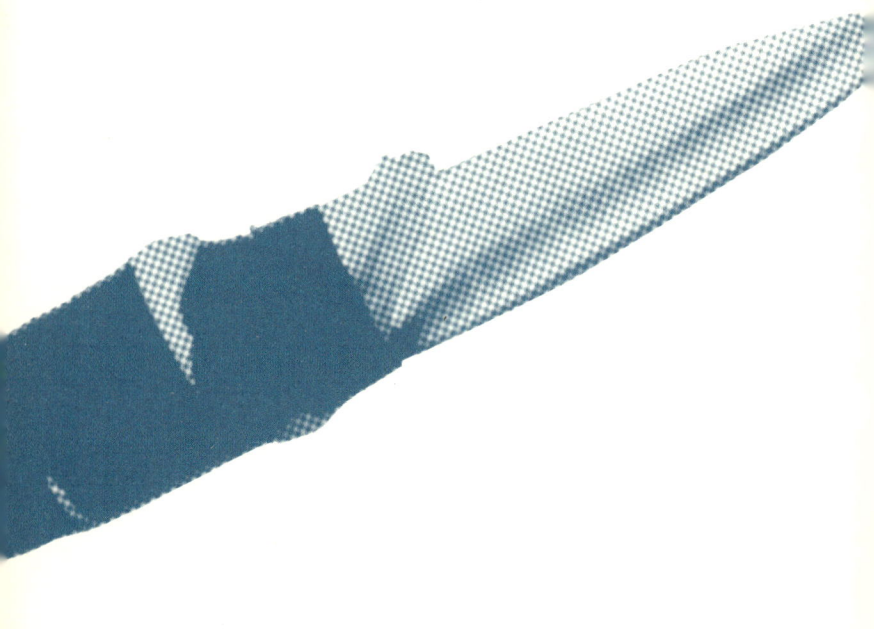

THE WEED MACAROONS

So, rather than put a recipe for macaroons, which you can find easily online, we figured we'd give you the keys to the kingdom. Your highness. With the below recipe you can turn butter into weed and make macaroons or even matzoh brie.

WEED BUTTER

INGREDIENTS

Double boiler or two pots
1 pound unsalted butter (4 sticks / 2 cups)
¼ ounce to 1 ounce marijuana buds
Strainer or cheesecloth
Small container

DIRECTIONS

1. Using a double boiler (or two pots), melt the butter on low heat. If using two pots, fill the larger (bottom) pot with water and the smaller (top) pot with butter.
2. Once the butter has melted, add the weed.
3. Simmer on low heat for at least 30 minutes (stirring every 5 minutes). To extract more THC from your pot, simmer for 2 to 3 hours.
4. Let the melted pot butter cool for 5 to 10 minutes, then strain the pot butter using a strainer or cheesecloth into a small container.
5. Cover and refrigerate your pot butter until semi-solid (or as required by your recipe).

Please remember your door is open throughout Passover. So, Google your zip code and make sure this is legal in your 'hood.

NON-GROSS GEFILTE FISH

Gefilte fish can be OK, but it can also be disgusting. In Europe did you know they fry it?! It is incredible. Here's my grandmother-in-law Adele's recipe for fried gefilte fish. She's Scottish and one of the best cooks in the entire world. (I'm not sure what an electric fish fryer is, but just go for it.)

INGREDIENTS

1 pound Hake, Haddock, Whiting, or Cod (3 pounds assorted fish are needed)
2 onions
5 tablespoons matzoh meal
1 tablespoon salt
1 teaspoon white pepper
1 teaspoon sugar
3 large eggs
1 cup water

DIRECTIONS

Put eggs and seasonings in blender and then add minced fish and meal. Mix well. With wet hands, form into 20 to 24 balls of even size (you get the hang after a few years). Have dish or brown paper with fine matzoh meal and coat each flattened fish ball evenly. Fry in hot oil for approximately 5 minutes, turning on both sides. I use an electric fish fryer in the garden because it does smell the house out.

MUSIC

Music can be of great use while using *The Unorthodox Haggadah*.
For a dramatic flair, you could play some Itzhak Perlman violin stuff.
For something more adventurous, there's Prokofiev's *Peter and the Wolf*.
But, we recommend putting "Exodus" by Bob Marley on repeat for the whole night.

We'll post playlists on UnorthodoxHaggadah.com as well.

SHAREABLE MOMENTS

Fun, family-friendly stuff intended to help you understand the Exodus story and also to keep you from getting bored. We call these "shareable moments." If you feel inspired to take a picture or a little video you are encouraged to do so. But, don't be annoying. When we think you might be doing something worth capturing we'll put a little icon [X] to let you know you should whip out the ol' phone for a sec.

When you post stuff use the hashtag #Unorthodox, and you can join all the other families who are doing this right now.

PLACES *NOT* TO LOOK FOR THE AFIKOMAN

Make a list here and read it during the Seder. We'll let you know when.

1. _____
2. _____
3. _____
4. _____
5. _____
6. _____
7. _____
8. _____
9. _____
10. _____

IF YOU'RE SO INCLINED, DRAW A MAP BELOW.

Put X's over rooms people aren't allowed to enter. It's like a treasure map of your embarrassing household secrets.

SHOUT-OUTS

Nathan wants to give a big shout-out to Robyn Ziegler, Danielle Svetcov and the team at Levine Greenberg, his editor Patty Rice, Ashley Legiadre for the illustrations, Joe Schiappa for the jokes, Rabbi Dan Ain and the 92Y, Noise, Rob Shepardson and SS+K, Adam, Dawn and Scott for showing him how it works at the kid's table, Ghost B.C. for inspiring us all to innovate rituals, Julia Rosenblatt and her family for the initial inspiration for the book, and Jessica for being so funny, talented, good at instant messaging, and Jewish-ish.

Jessica would like to give a shout-out to Nick Boney and Nikki Albrecht for the food, support, and mini breaks, her family for raising her right, and Nathan for coming up with all the funny words and wanting more people to read them.

The Unorthodox Haggadah copyright © 2015 by Nathan Phillips. All rights reserved. Printed in China. No part of this book may be used or reproduced in any manner whatsoever without written permission except in the case of reprints in the context of reviews.

Andrews McMeel Publishing, LLC
an Andrews McMeel Universal company
1130 Walnut Street, Kansas City, Missouri 64106

www.andrewsmcmeel.com

15 16 17 18 19 SDB 10 9 8 7 6 5 4 3 2 1

ISBN: 978-1-4494-6031-0

Library of Congress Control Number: 2014946029

This book is intended solely for entertainment purposes. The Publisher does not endorse or condone violating the law and does not intend to encourage or promote the illegal use of marijuana. Readers' use of the content in this book is at their own risk. The Publisher does not warrant or guarantee the accuracy or completeness of any information herein, and in no event will the Publisher be liable for any loss or damage whatsoever arising from the use of the information in this book.

ATTENTION: SCHOOLS AND BUSINESSES

Andrews McMeel books are available at quantity discounts with bulk purchase for educational, business, or sales promotional use. For information, please e-mail the Andrews McMeel Publishing Special Sales Department:
specialsales@amuniversal.com.